MONSTER MAKER

& other poems

D.L. Huff

Illustrated by Courtenay Rushing

ISBN 978-1-63630-703-9 (Paperback)
ISBN 978-1-63630-704-6 (Hardcover)
ISBN 978-1-63630-705-3 (Digital)

Covenant Books, Inc.
11661 Hwy 707
Murrells Inlet, SC 29576
www.covenantbooks.com

Contents

The Dentist's Apprentice

I went to the dentist to see his apprentice, because the good doctor was out.
But he was quite hairy and started to scare me
So I would not smile, I'd just pout.

And while at the dentist to see the apprentice,
    he seemed a good bit confused.
When he heard me blurbing that his hair was disturbing
I must say...he was NOT amused.

I went to the dentist to see his apprentice, and
    now have great reason for grief.
Though holes, canals neither, he dosed me with ether,
And pulled out all of my teeth.

I went to the dentist
To see his apprentice;
Now my friends
They all find it quite funny.
For when I am tickled,
Made happy or giggle
My smile is nothing but gummy.

Spider Bath

There's a spider perched next to my tub;
He must be feeling dirty.
I've warned him not to join me
Several times now
(I'd guess thirty).

He's glared at me
With many eyes–
More eyes than
    I can tell.
But it quite appears
    to me,
Chagrinned:
His ears don't
    work too well.

I don't mind helping
    scrub him,
But don't hold out much hope.
With all those hairy parts and legs...
I think I'm short on soap.

My Uncle and My Ant

My uncle and my ant
Have quite the odd romance;
They don't see eye-to-eye
In many cases.

But they'll stroll around the park
For long hours after dark,
Laughing at the looks
On people's faces.

When at last their walk is through,
Their favorite thing to do
Is to snuggle on the most
crowd-filled benches.

My uncle puckers up, but he's
always out of luck.
For my ant, she doesn't kiss
She only pinches.

The Hungry Mommy

One day my mom was hungry
Quite famished, if you please.
And we couldn't drive to the grocery store 'cause my daddy had her keys.

She opened up our giant fridge (she found nothing there).
She ransacked all the cupboards next,
But all of them were bare.

She looked inside the cabinets;
She only found some tea.
She screamed
"I need something to eat!"
And then she turned
    To me.

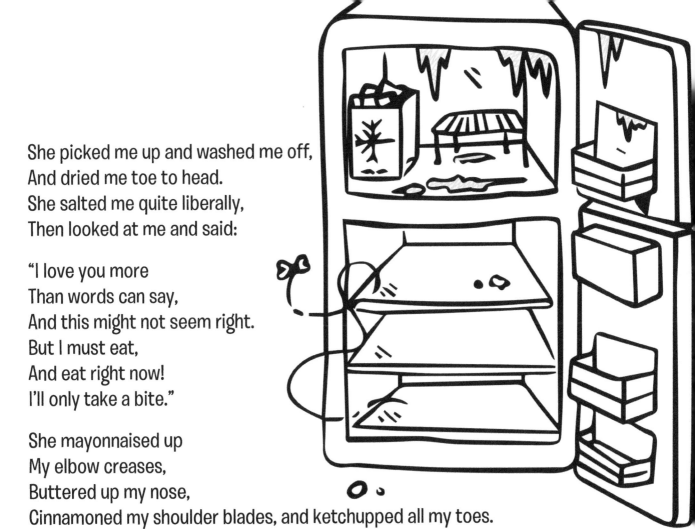

She picked me up and washed me off,
And dried me toe to head.
She salted me quite liberally,
Then looked at me and said:

"I love you more
Than words can say,
And this might not seem right.
But I must eat,
And eat right now!
I'll only take a bite."

She mayonnaised up
My elbow creases,
Buttered up my nose,
Cinnamoned my shoulder blades, and ketchupped all my toes.

She brushed my ribs with barbecue sauce, squirted mustard on my shins,
Dunked my thumbs in cold hot fudge...
Sprinkled sugar on my chin.

"But, Mom," I said, "What did I do?
I've been so good today.
I've done everything you asked of me, and in a timely way.

"I cleaned my room right after lunch; I picked up all my toys.
And when you were on the phone with Dad,
I didn't make ANY noise.

"I didn't talk back, or whine or fuss, or watch too much TV.
I did ALL of my homework;
I even brushed my teeth!"

To that, my mommy answered me
With a voice so soft and sweet,
"My Dear, you have been good today
You were good enough to eat."

6

Squeakers

Will my sneakers still be sneaky
Since I left them in the rain?

Will I leave tracks on the carpet?
And in the kitchen...puddles? Stains?

Will my friends all hear me coming?
Will they know from whence I came?

Some people think I'm crazy, but to me, it's all the same,
Cause I have brand-new SQUEAKERS now,
So why would I complain?

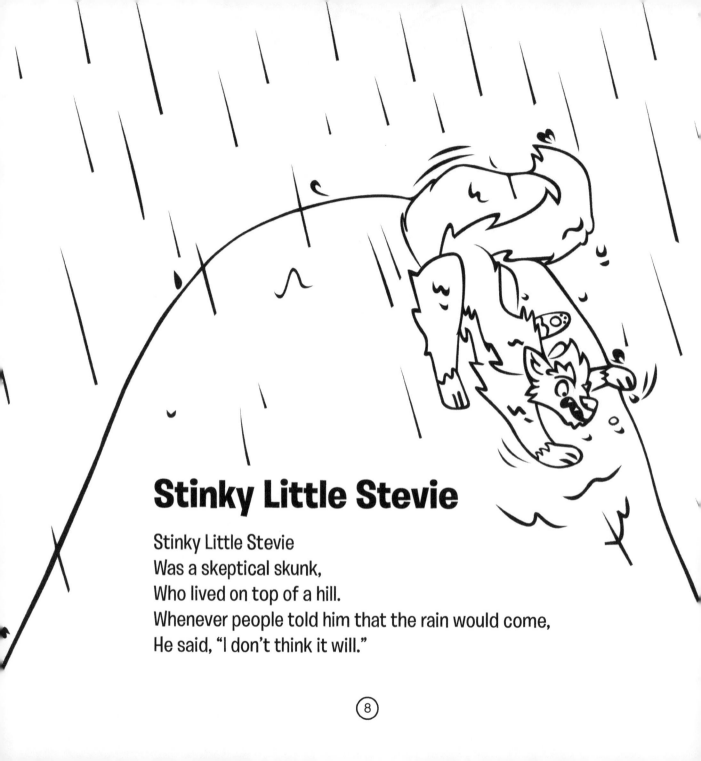

Stinky Little Stevie

Stinky Little Stevie
Was a skeptical skunk,
Who lived on top of a hill.
Whenever people told him that the rain would come,
He said, "I don't think it will."

But then one summer afternoon the sky grew dark,
The rain came tumbling down.
And Stinky Little Stevie, the skeptical skunk
Was washed right into town.

Now Stinky Little Stevie, the skeptical skunk
Learned his lesson well.
He married Tina Turtle by the side of the pond
And lives inside her shell.

The Things I Think

I think the sea is human.
In fact, she's my best friend,
And we can sit and talk
For days and days.

But she's a wee bit different
When our chats begin and end
It's never "Hi" or "Bye,"
　　　Just lots of waves.

10

I think that clouds are bubbles, full of air and gas and such.
They choose to float (They're much too high to hop).

But they're all leaking backwards;
Oh, so slowly, just a touch.
And when they're full,
   They simply pop, then drop.

I think the forest is friendly when the weather's nice and warm.
He wishes he could give us each a squeeze.

During spring and summer, he just turns on all the charm
And when it's getting chilly
   Well...he leaves.

I think water has poor balance; yes, the truth, it must be told:
It splashes past and tries to fool us all.

It churns down creeks and rivers,
'Round the bends and twists and folds.
And when it gets too steep,
   The water falls.

Ghost in the Toaster

There's a ghost inside my toaster...an unseen, fiendish beast.
He likes his home quite warmish, and must love the smell of yeast.

He taunts me with the timer, which I know now not to trust,
Since he ejects at leisure my delicious bread and crust.

I've tried priest, charm, and séance,
To make the cruel ghoul stop.
For he never utters "BOO!," Oh, no,
My toaster ghost says "POP!"

Friends wait outside at breakfast,
Chuckling as I scream and run.
They just can't wait to fill their plates
'Cause they know the toast is done.

13

Monster Maker

I have a Monster Maker.
I ordered it online.
It came in ninety pieces,
And assembly took some time.

The concept is quite simple:
Put random items in.
Out comes a
Custom monster
Sure to scare
Your sister's friends.

Instructions were
    in German,
All the parts in Japanese.
By the time they were deciphered, I had scuffed up both my knees.

But once I had it working,
Couldn't wait for my first test.
I knew it might take time, though, to find out what "monsters" best.

I dropped in beans and tuna, wanting something nasty, vicious.
What came out was soft and stinky
(But it tasted quite delicious.)

Next came mums and lilies,
A few cobwebs from the attic.
Out popped a thing not scary,
And it smelled, ummm...well...fantastic.

Third, a whoopee cushion,
Marshmallows and sweet tea.
It made the oddest noises,
But was cute as cute can be.

So now I rent my service
Making strange pets large and small.
If you need a thing not-frightening,
        PLEASE,
                Feel free to call.

Ticklish

My sister likes to poke me.
She does it every day.
She knows that I'm quite ticklish, and she thinks that it's okay.

She likes to hear me giggle,
And she loves to see me twitch.
(I'm sure I'd do the same thing if our tickliness were switched.)

She always pokes me gently.
No, she never leaves a bruise.
But she always uses girlie stuff like dolls and high-heel shoes.

My friend asked me this question
And it really made me think:
If I'm poked by too many girlie things,
    Will I end up tickled pink?

Momkey

Our mother is quite different
Since our visit to the zoo.
We've noticed several changes in
The things she needs to do.

We were passing by the monkey house
When we saw our mommy smile.
She stood and watched them for a bit
Then said, "I like their style."

Dad says she's fine in brown, fur-lined,
Prehensile-tailed new jammas,
But she walks with a bounce,
Her hands held high, and will only eat bananas.

She still peeks in post-breakfast-time to make sure we brush our teeth
And if we're slow, she makes us go with a terrible, high-pitched screech.

There's still a lunch packed every day before the bus comes 'round.
But it's no longer ham or PBJ, just a stick for termite mounds.

At dinnertime, we usually find her high up in a tree.
And she'll toss us down a bug or two
    (Sometimes even three).

She still comes up, yes, every night, to tuck us in to bed,
But she doesn't walk upstairs or down
She swings from the lights instead.

In light of all these differences,
We thought we'd
    change her name.
So we all call her
"Momkey" now...
    And love her,
        just the same.

The Great Cheese Debate

By the ambient light of a large, well-stocked fridge,
That someone left open, just more than a smidge...

The shelves overflowing with all kinds of cheese
(And the temp set just right, so their edges don't freeze).

It started, quite strangely, with a smirk from the string,
Who decided–on a whim–to make his case to be king.

The others were shocked, they'd never witnessed such gall,
Why would any cheese think he could rule over all?

But the cheeses decided that dark, fateful night,
To crown one cheese sovereign (by vote, not birthright).

Each was invited to make his case for the throne.
The first to be heard was Signore Provolone.
His rambling was met with some not-so-nice words;
And a chorus of cackles from the oft-sour curds.

Then this comment came, right out of the bleu:
"I may not be best, sir,
        ...But I'm better than YOU!"

Next came the cottage, who was cute, but points hollow.
Then the cream, a smooth talker...a right tough act to follow.

Next Muenster, whose roarings all thought were absurd;
Then parmesan (with a voice that quite grated on nerves).

Both queso and nacho had similar spins,
Yet seemed much too gooey to have a real chance to win.

The Limburger's pitch: Better than one might think.
Still, everyone thought,
        As a king, he would stink.

Gruyere took the stage with a je ne sais quoi.
Yet, not speaking French, no one gave him much thought.

Two Jacks, Colby, Pepper, gave their speeches last;
Before feta insisted that votes must be cast.

A cacophony of calls came,
    One half, then two thirds.
(The Swiss remained neutral,
Not saying a word.
Unmistakably acting
"Holier than thou"),
While the others continued
To scream for the crown.

    Mr. Cheddar, however, was one quite sharp fella.
    He suggested the title be Sir Mozzarella's.
    A gentleman's cheese, of high, noble line.
    With a quiet demeanor,
        And a taste quite refined.

        The screams, they receded;
        Everyone seemed quite pleased.
        So they crowned him,
            Forevermore called...

The Big Cheese!

Hairy Brain

My hair is growing backwards, and it's tickling my brain.
It kind of makes me giggle, but it causes me no pain.

I have to see a surgeon when I need a little trim,
I know a Dr. Cutter, though...(I'll get a deal from him).

If it gets to be a problem and fuzzy seems my mind,
I'll just flip my bald scalp inside out
And surely will be fine.

Yawning Trouble

My friend cannot stop yawning,
Stretching arms and sleepy eyes.
A hiccup might be subtle, but these yawns he can't disguise.

His voice it sounds so silly.
All his words are yawn-erized.
If he can't stop yawning, though, at least he can catch flies.

The Tidy Toilet

There once was a toilet
That thought if he boiled it
His water would always be clean.

He tried, that poor fellow,
But his teeth are still yellow...
(I think you know what I mean).

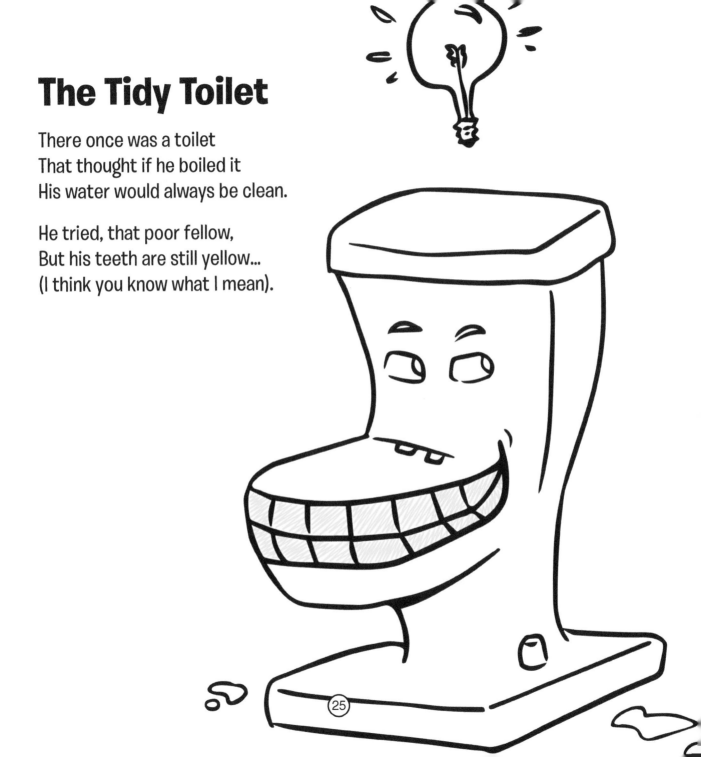

The Burping Banana

I knew a banana
Who was quite often gassy.
He lived in a bowl that was beautifully glassy.

His dish-mates complained,
For he never refrained.
He refused quite intently all squelching.

They continued to ask
For they so loved their glass,
Which was quite often fogged by his belching.

To their utter dismay
He got worse every day,
This unpopular gaseous fruit.

They fussed and they groaned,
But to their loud moans
        He replied:
            "Would you rather me toot?"

About the Author

The son of a minister and an English teacher, D. L. Huff was born and raised in Alabama and developed a tremendous love of language incredibly early in life. He moved to the Atlanta, Georgia, area in his mid-twenties, and it was there that he met his wife, Amy. The two settled down and started a family, but Huff never lost his passion for writing and poetry. Once his children were old enough to enjoy and appreciate wordplay and associated silliness, Huff decided to pursue poetry more seriously. Inspired–and sometimes assisted–by his kids (affectionately referred to as "The Hufflings"), he amassed a fairly sizable collection of poems and is now ready to share his work with a larger audience. After an exhaustive search to find "the perfect illustrator," Huff partnered with the young and extraordinarily talented Courtenay Rushing and has assembled his first collection, entitled *Monster Maker & Other Poems.* Rushing is an Atlanta-area native, and her style both complements and completes the collection seamlessly. The two of them are tremendously excited about creating more family-friendly collections and books in the years to come.

CPSIA information can be obtained
at www.ICGtesting.com
Printed in the USA
LVHW072034030621
689237LV00018B/1279